Contents

Dickens and his world 4

Why did Dickens write *Oliver Twist?* 10

Victorian life 20

Dickens and his city... 30

Changing times 36

After *Oliver Twist* 42

Timeline 50

Further Information.. 52

Glossary... 54

Index... 56

Some words are shown in bold, **like this**. You can find out what they mean by looking in the glossary.

Dickens and his world

Charles Dickens was one of the greatest English novelists of the 1800s. He lived through the first half of "the Victorian Age". The period from 1837–1901 is named after Britain's Queen Victoria who reigned at that time. Dickens became a celebrity as a young writer. His early novels, such as *Oliver Twist*, appeared in monthly instalments in magazines. People rushed to buy each issue to find out what happened next. Dickens' books have been translated into many languages, and turned into films and television dramas. Many of the characters he created, including Mr Pickwick, Mr Micawber, Scrooge, Fagin, and Oliver Twist himself are familiar to people who have never read the books in which they feature.

Dickens the celebrity

In Dickens' time, there were no television chat shows for famous authors to appear on, but many people saw him because he toured widely, giving dramatic readings from his books. Had he not become a writer, Dickens, who loved the theatre, might well have been a professional actor. He visited France, Canada, and the United States, where his books also sold well. Dickens was a success because he wrote great stories with a host of characters – both amusing and terrifying – and because he was not afraid to tackle serious issues of his time.

A painting by William Powell Frith (1819–1909) shows Dickens at his desk. Dickens normally wrote very quickly, stopping every so often to walk around or act a character in front of the mirror.

HISTORY IN LITERATURE

THE STORY BEHIND...

CHARLES DICKENS'
OLIVER TWIST

Brian Williams

Heinemann

www.heinemann.co.uk/library
Visit our website to find out more information about Heinemann Library books.

To order:

 Phone 44 (0) 1865 888066

 Send a fax to 44 (0) 1865 314091

 Visit the Heinemann Bookshop at www.heinemann.co.uk/library to
browse our catalogue and order online.

First published in Great Britain by
Heinemann Library, Halley Court, Jordan Hill,
Oxford, OX2 8EJ, part of Harcourt Education.
Heinemann is a registered trademark of
Harcourt Education Ltd.

© Harcourt Education Ltd 2007
First published in paperback in 2008
The moral right of the proprietor has
been asserted.

Editorial: Louise Galpine, Lucy Beevor,
and Rosie Gordon
Design: Richard Parker and Manhattan Design
Maps: International Mapping
Picture Research: Melissa Allison
and Ginny Stroud-Lewis
Production: Vicki Fitzgerald
Originated by Modern Age
Printed and bound in China by Leo Paper Group

13 digit ISBN 978 0 431 08174 8 (hardback)
11 10 09 08 07
10 9 8 7 6 5 4 3 2 1

13 digit ISBN 978 0 431 08191 5 (paperback)
12 11 10 09 08
10 9 8 7 6 5 4 3 2 1

British Library Cataloguing in Publication Data
Williams, Brian, 1943-   The story behind Oliver
Twist. - (History in literature)
 823.8
A full catalogue record for this book is available
from the British Library.

Acknowledgements
The publisher would like to thank the
following for permission to reproduce
photographs: **p. 8**, Alamy Images/Robert Harding
Picture Library Ltd; **p. 38**, Alamy/Mary Evans
Picture Library; **p. 42**, Corbis; **p. 39**, Corbis/Fine
Art Photographic Library; **p. 33**, Corbis/Hulton-
Deutsch Collection; **pp. 22, 25, 30, 37, 41, 45,
47, 48** Getty Images/Hulton Archive; **p. 6**, Getty
Images/Time Life Pictures; **p. 44**, Illustrated
London News; **pp. 5, 9, 10, 11 12, 13, 15, 18, 20,
23, 24, 26, 27, 35, 34, 43, 46, 49**, Mary Evans
Picture Library; **p. 29**, The Bridgeman Art Library/
Private Collection, The Stapleton Collection; **p.
19**, The Bridgeman Art Library/ © Dickens House
Museum, London, UK; **pp. 14, 32**, The
Bridgeman Art Library/ © Guildhall Library,
Corporation of London, UK; **p. 7**, The Bridgeman
Art Library/ Dickens House Museum, London,
UK; **pp. 16, 17**, The Bridgeman Art Library/Private
Collection; **p. 21**, The Bridgeman Art Library/
Private Collection, © Ackermann and Johnson
Ltd, London, UK; **p. 40**, The Bridgeman Art
Library/Private Collection, The Stapleton
Collection; **p. 4**, The Bridgeman Art Library/
Victoria & Albert Museum, London, UK.
Cover: Getty Images/ Hulton Archive. Cover
background: istockphoto.com/ Chris Crafter.

Every effort has been made to contact
copyright holders of any material
reproduced in this book. Any omissions
will be rectified in subsequent printings
if notice is given to the publishers.

Disclaimer

Over London by Rail is an engraving of London houses in the 1830s, by the French artist Gustave Doré. London was then the biggest city in the world. Rows of small brick houses were built alongside the railways which carried people and goods from all over Britain into the crowded, smoky capital city.

Dickens and a time of change

Dickens lived through an age of tremendous social and scientific change, brought about by the **Industrial Revolution**. Britain was rapidly transforming from a green land of farms to an industrial nation of factories and cities. By the 1800s, the new machine age was spreading to other nations, too, particularly the United States, France, and Germany. A feature of the new age was the rapid growth of cities such as London.

In *Oliver Twist*, Dickens wrote about London's dark underworld – about the poor, the street children, thieves, and **prostitutes**, who roamed the back alleys. Cruelty and injustice made Dickens angry, especially when children were abused and abandoned. *Oliver Twist* was his first protest on behalf of the weak and innocent.

"What manner of life is that which is described in these pages…?" Dickens wrote in a preface to *Oliver Twist*. He answered his own question; the story is about:

> *the everyday existence of a Thief… The cold wet shelterless midnight streets of London; the foul and frowsy dens where vice is closely packed.*

Dickens with his daughters Mamie and Katie, photographed in the family country home, Gad's Hill Place in Kent. Although his marriage ended unhappily, Dickens had a loving relationship with his children.

What was Dickens like?

Dickens' friend and **biographer**, John Forster, said he was "the best and most rapid reporter ever known", and added that he had never seen the writer work so late at night, as when racing to finish *Oliver Twist*. When Dickens died, worn out at the age of 58, his 16th novel unfinished, he had also written many shorter pieces, and edited two weekly journals.

Why is Dickens so admired?

Writer Peter Ackroyd has said that, "Dickens captured the soul of the English people." Dickens' gallery of characters were drawn from his observation of life. Often his novels read like plays. This helps them transfer easily, often brilliantly, to the stage, film, and television. This adaptability has helped Dickens to gain his reputation as one of the world's most popular writers. In his lifetime, Dickens was a celebrity. People stopped him in the street to thank him for the pleasure his books had given them. Some people wept and even fainted during his dramatic public readings – one of which was the death of Nancy, from *Oliver Twist*.

DICKENS THE ACTOR

"...if that man would go upon the stage, he would make his £20,000 a year", commented William Makepeace Thackeray an English writer whose bestselling novel Vanity Fair was published in 1847–1848, like Oliver Twist, in monthly parts. Thackeray said this after watching one of Dickens' private theatrical shows. Dickens once considered becoming a professional actor, and loved to act in his own amateur productions.

Though Dickens' marriage became unhappy, he was fond of his ten children. He amused them with tricks, games, and play-acting, but also sometimes ignored them when he was deep in thought. He would often write in a corner of the room while visitors chatted around the fire. Dickens was a public figure, and a friend of leading writers, actors, and politicians. He also gave support to **reformers** and had a strong **social conscience**.

The background to *Oliver Twist*

By writing *Oliver Twist*, Dickens hoped to highlight the problems of children on the streets. The book's subtitle was "The Parish Boy's Progress". Every town in Britain had at least one **parish workhouse** for abandoned children such as Oliver, for the poor, the sick, and the old. But the old parish system of "relief", or welfare, could not cope with growing numbers of poor people. Parishes in the southern states of the United States also served as church and local government districts, but in US cities poverty was less of a problem at this time, since the Industrial Revolution had still to make its full impact on the country. In 1834, government changes to the **Poor Law**, the British system for helping the poor, made life even harder for people living in poverty.

Charles Dickens by Daniel Maclise (1839). The young rising star of the London literary world is elegantly dressed and stylish. Despite his early success, Dickens never stopped working at a hectic pace, as if fearful of failure.

Dickens' early life

Charles John Huffam Dickens was born near Portsmouth, on the south coast of England, on 7 February 1812. Portsmouth was the home of the British navy, and in 1812 Britain was at war, not only with France, but also with the United States.

Dickens' father John worked as a Navy clerk. He and his wife Elizabeth had eight children, of whom Charles was their eldest son. Although he was kindly and amusing, John Dickens was not very successful. He behaved as though he had money, but never had enough to send his children to school regularly. Mrs Dickens had ambitions. She tried to start her own school, but no pupils came.

In 1816, John Dickens got work as a clerk in the naval dockyard at Chatham in Kent. Life was good until 1822 when the family moved to London. Around this time Charles' baby sister Harriet died from **smallpox**. Charles, who was at school in Kent, arrived in London after his family. He travelled alone in a **stagecoach**, watching the rain and eating sandwiches amid the smell of damp straw.

This is the house where Dickens was born. It is now a museum in his memory, but was originally 1 Mile End Terrace, Landport, Portsmouth.

Dickens in London

Dickens' new home – for parents, five children, a servant, and a lodger – was a small house, with four rooms and a basement, in Camden Town, part of London. John Dickens slid into so much debt that Charles was sent to work in Warren's Warehouse, a rat-infested factory overlooking the River Thames. The factory made and sold "blacking" to clean fire grates. His job, which he hated, was sealing and labelling jars of the stuff. Further disgrace came when his father was jailed for six months in the Marshalsea prison, for not paying his bills. Dickens later wrote about the prison in his novel *Little Dorrit*.

In 1824 the family fortunes improved enough to pay for three years' schooling for Charles. In 1827, at the age of fifteen, he left school to work in a law office. He hated it, and seldom had a good word to say about lawyers in his books! Determined to improve himself, he walked to the British Museum to study. Charles taught himself shorthand, a skill that earned him a job as a reporter on Parliament. In his work as a journalist, he also travelled around England by stagecoach, and began to make notes for stories he called "sketches".

The young writer

Dickens' first story was published in 1833, anonymously, before he chose the **pen-name** "Boz". In April 1836, he married Catherine Hogarth, the daughter of a Scottish music critic and colleague on the *Morning Chronicle* newspaper. In November that year, Dickens agreed with the publisher Richard Bentley to edit a monthly magazine and write stories for it. His first effort was a comic **serial**, *The Pickwick Papers*. Sales were fantastic – from 400 copies for Episode 1 to 40,000 for Episode 15. Dickens was a success. Yet even as he worked late into the night on the next instalment of *Pickwick*, he was also scribbling a new book, *Oliver Twist*. This was to be a very different story.

John Dickens was a kind father, but a poor manager of the family finances. The character of Mr Micawber in *David Copperfield* is often thought to represent Mr Dickens.

WORKING CHILDREN

*Work in the blacking factory was **squalid**, dirty, and boring. Charles hated both the work and his workmates because he thought they were "common". The experience at Warren's Warehouse opened his eyes to the world of child labour. In the early 1800s, most children worked either on farms, alongside their parents, or in factories, mills, and mines. Some of these children were as young as five. Small boys swept chimneys by scrambling up inside them to sweep them, or rooted in **privies** and river mud for lost jewellery and scrap metal.*

Why did Dickens write *Oliver Twist*?

Why did Dickens write his story of an orphaned boy who falls in with London criminals? Firstly, because he had a contract with Richard Bentley to write fourteen pages of story each month. Secondly, he realized that newspaper coverage of the new Poor Law Amendment Act made it a topical issue. Thirdly, the theme of a "lost child" was one he knew well; although he tended to exaggerate the hardships of his own childhood, childhood misery felt real to him.

In Chapter Three of *Oliver Twist*, the magistrate takes pity on Oliver, and decides not to condemn him to the terrible life of a "chimney boy".

The poverty issue

In the 1800s, people with no money relied on welfare, from charity, and a system of local parish "handouts" dating from the 1500s. For homeless youngsters, crime often seemed the only escape from poverty. But many better-off people knew nothing of the criminal underworld. In the *Quarterly Review* critic Robert Ford wrote that *Oliver Twist* "opens a new world to thousands born and bred in the same city ... for the one half of mankind lives without knowing how the other half dies".

TWO NATIONS?

Writing in 1829, historian Thomas Carlyle said that his was "the Mechanical Age". Machines were replacing men, because they were faster, cheaper, and needed no rest. Carlyle saw two nations in the new industrial Britain: the rich and poor, the "Dandies and Drudges". Dickens saw the same division on the streets of London, but was less gloomy about the future than Carlyle.

Dickens had spent many hours in London's streets and squares, and he knew its darker secrets. Despite the misery he had seen, Dickens was hopeful. In the book, he makes much of small acts of generosity: a roadside gate-keeper gives Oliver bread and cheese, Mr Brownlow takes the ragged street-urchin (homeless child) into his home, Mrs Bedwin mothers him back to health, and even Fagin cooks sausages for his boys.

Determined to shock

By sending an orphan character into the backstreets of London, Dickens could tackle the themes that most interested him, however shocking. In a preface to *Oliver Twist*, he wrote that he had little time for people "so refined" that they "cannot bear the contemplation of such horrors". He went on, "I had no respect for their opinion, good or bad; did not covet [seek] their approval; and did not write for their amusement."

SEND THE KIDS TO WORK

Poor families were forced to send young children to work, as they desperately needed extra wages. In 1832, 40 per cent of factory workers in the New England region of America (the six eastern states of Connecticut, Maine, Massachusetts, New Hampshire, Rhode Island and Vermont) were aged seven to sixteen. The situation was even worse in Britain. Until a law change in 1833, many children were working more than 48 hours a week.

Holborn Viaduct in London, with St Paul's cathedral behind. A steam train passes over a street jammed with horse-drawn vehicles. Away from the noise and dirt of the City and River Thames, London still had green fields and villages, such as Pentonville, where Mr Brownlow lives on a "quiet, shady street".

OLIVER ASKS FOR MORE

The scene in Chapter Two where Oliver asks for more gruel is the most familiar episode in the book. Mr Bumble brings him before the workhouse "board", or managers, who are shocked. One of them asks indignantly:
"Do I understand that he asked for more, after he had eaten the supper allotted by the dietary [the ration]?'
'He did, sir' replied Bumble.
'That boy will be hung,' said the gentleman in the white waistcoat."

The plot of *Oliver Twist*

The story begins with a situation familiar in Victorian stories: a woman is abandoned by the father of her child, and dies after her baby's birth. The orphan child is named Oliver Twist and raised by a cruel foster-mother, Mrs Mann. At the age of nine, he is taken to the **workhouse**. "Wretched as were the little companions in misery he was leaving behind, they were the only friends he had ever known; and a sense of his loneliness in the great, wide world, sank into the child's heart for the first time."

Oliver runs away

In the workhouse, Oliver causes anger by asking for a second helping of gruel (a thin porridge). The result is that Mr Bumble, the **beadle**, "sells" him to work for the undertaker (funeral director) Mr Sowerberry. To escape the Sowerberry family and their bullying **apprentice** Noah Claypole, Oliver runs away to London.

Here, hungry and homeless, he meets the street thief Jack Dawkins, known as "The Artful Dodger".

Two offers of "rescue"

The Dodger leads Oliver to a den of boy-thieves, led by Fagin, an old Jewish man, who organizes thefts and then sells the stolen goods. At first, Fagin treats Oliver kindly, though it turns out that his **motives** are dark. Oliver is given a bed and food, but also taught to pick people's pockets and steal silk handkerchiefs in what he thinks is a game. On the streets, he soon realizes what the young thieves are up to. When the Dodger steals a handkerchief and runs, Oliver runs too, but is caught. He is rescued when a witness clears him. Mr Brownlow, the old gentleman whose pocket was picked, takes Oliver home to be cared for by the motherly housekeeper Mrs Bedwin. Mr Brownlow has a picture of a young woman. Unknown to Oliver, it is a painting of his dead mother.

"Delighted to see you looking so well, my dear", says Fagin as Oliver is recaptured by the gang. This illustration from Chapter Sixteen of the novel was drawn by George Cruikshank (1792-1878), the artist who did all the pictures for the first edition of *Oliver Twist*. Dickens sent him sections of text, and sometimes suggested changes to the sketches Cruikshank sent back.

The plot thickens

The second half of the book introduces Mrs Maylie and her son Harry, Mrs Maylie's niece Rose, and the villain Monks. Monks is Oliver's half-brother, and has bribed Fagin to trap Oliver into crime, and so cheat him out of a **legacy**. Recaptured by Fagin's gang, Oliver is "loaned" to the burglar Bill Sikes. The plot against Oliver fails when he is shot during an attempted robbery, and taken in by the Maylies.

Murder and endings

Nancy, a prostitute and Sikes' girlfriend, learns about the plot between Fagin and Monks, and tells Rose Maylie in secret. But Sikes discovers Nancy's "treachery" and murders her in a fit of rage. Fagin is arrested, the gang scatters, and Sikes falls to his death while fleeing from the police. Fagin is sentenced to hang. Oliver visits him in prison and prays for his forgiveness. Rose, who is discovered to be Oliver's aunt, marries Harry Maylie. Mr Brownlow adopts Oliver as his son. Monks leaves the country in disgrace. Mr Bumble the beadle ends up in the workhouse himself, unhappily married to a nagging wife.

FAGIN AND ANTI-JEWISH FEELING

Fagin is Jewish. Like other minorities in Victorian Britain, such as Catholics, Jewish people often faced racial and religious intolerance. An 1830s Report of the Society for the Suppression of Mendicity [begging] in the British Quarterly Review accused some Jewish people in Britain of being criminals: "if a robbery is effected, the property is hid till a Jew is found and a bargain is then made." This suggested that Jews were known for buying stolen goods from thieves.

The author and his book

Dickens wrote that he "saw no reason why the dregs of life [the underclass and street-crooks]...should not serve the purpose of a moral." The new Poor Law of 1834 was at first welcomed as an improvement by social reformers, but soon people were changing their minds. Dr Thomas Arnold of Rugby School – England's most famous head teacher and a man Dickens admired – called the new law "wise and just", but by 1839 Arnold decided it had done more harm than good. Dickens, and *Oliver Twist*, had helped change the public mood.

London's River Thames was a source of endless inspiration and interest to Dickens. This lithograph by William Parrott (1813–1869) shows a peaceful view of the river near Westminster.

Memories

Oliver Twist is a very personal book. Though it is wrong to assume that the young Dickens is part of the character of Oliver, the writer did keep a child's eye view of the world. He never forgot the happiest years of his childhood, in Chatham, where his home overlooked a hayfield and a river bustling with ships. He later wrote: "it was a mistake to fancy children ever forgot anything". Just as powerful were later memories of working ten hours a day in Warren's Warehouse. "No words can express the secret agony of my soul..." was how he described that experience.

THE REAL FAGIN

Dickens had met a boy named Bob Fagin at the blacking factory. Bob Fagin was an orphan and a friend, but Dickens felt ashamed at mixing with such a "common" boy. When Bob Fagin walked home with him one evening, Dickens pretended he lived in a fine house. He walked up to the door, waved goodbye to his friend – then sneaked away.

FAMILY LIFE

*Dickens **idealized** the family, though his own family life was far from perfect. Mr Brownlow, Mrs Bedwin, and the Maylies represent the ideal "family values". They are kind, caring, and comforting. Their homes are like islands in the rough seas of the underworld into which Oliver is tossed. Mr Brownlow's home is described in Chapter Fourteen: "Everything was so quiet, and neat and orderly; everybody was kind and gentle...it seemed like Heaven itself."*

While writing *Oliver Twist*, Dickens was saddened by the sudden death of his sister-in-law, Mary Hogarth, who was only seventeen years old. The character of Rose Maylie is probably based on Mary. In *Oliver Twist*, Rose Maylie is introduced as a person "... in the lovely bloom and springtime of womanhood ... so pure and beautiful; that earth seemed not her element, nor its rough creatures her fit companions." Her later illness "mirrors" the real illness of Mary Hogarth – except that Rose recovers.

The way he wrote

Dickens wrote quickly, to keep up the monthly episodes. As a serial-writer, he had to think up a "climax" for each instalment to keep the reader in suspense for the next episode. Finally, at the end of the novel, villains are sent packing and the "good" characters find their happy endings. We are not told what becomes of Oliver as an adult, or whether his childhood experiences scarred him in any way – a topic that might interest a modern writer.

A drawing by Daniel Maclise of Dickens with his wife Catherine and her sister Georgina. She came to live with the couple in 1842, the year this drawing was made. Maclise became famous for a series of portraits of literary celebrities.

A 19th-century textile mill. Millions of men, women and children went to work in factories. Most factories and mills were dirty, noisy and dangerous places where workers toiled long hours for low wages.

Dickens in his time

Oliver Twist appeared at a time when some people feared that Britain might be on the verge of political **revolution**. Queen Victoria was a new queen, and previous monarchs had not been much liked or respected. The gap between rich and poor was getting bigger, and this sparked fears of unrest. "They are like two nations that have no contact or sympathy", wrote Benjamin Disraeli in 1846, talking about the rich and poor.

The reform movement

In Britain, reformers campaigned for a fairer voting system, encouraged by the **Reform** Act that was made law in 1832. The Reform Act gave more people the right to vote. But even after this change in the law, many people in Britain still had no vote, and no say in government. That is why the **Chartist** movement of 1838, with its demands that all adult males should have the right to vote, attracted wide support with petitions and demonstrations.

New technology helped the reformers. Steam-driven printing presses made it cheaper, and quicker, to print newspapers, magazines, and books. With this technology, writers could reach an ever-growing readership to reveal social problems, such as prostitution, crime, and child labour. In the 1830s, the first laws were passed to control the employment of child workers in factories, mills, and mines. The British Factory Act of 1833 barred the employment of children under nine years old, and a similar law in Massachusetts in 1836 was the first state law in the United States to restrict child labour.

To the new world

Many poor people in Europe looked westward for a new life in the United States. Ships took settlers across the ocean. From eastern cities, such as New York City, thousands of migrants headed along wagon trails to the West. At the time of *Oliver Twist*, the United States had only around ten million people – half the population of Britain – but it was growing fast.

In 1838 *Sirius* was the first ship to provide regular steam crossings from Britain to the United States. In 1842, Dickens travelled there by steamer. However, the rough voyage made him decide to return by a slower sailing ship. Dickens was quickly a favourite with American readers. He did not enjoy this first visit, and was rather rude about Americans, but changed his mind later.

A locomotive on the Liverpool and Manchester Railway in 1831, the year after it opened. The first passenger railway to use steam power, it **pioneered** a new era that transformed both landscape and society.

Benjamin Disraeli (1804–1881)

Benjamin Disraeli was a British politician of Italian-Jewish origins. He was brought up as a Christian to avoid anti-Jewish discrimination: until 1858, no Jewish person could be a British Member of Parliament. Disraeli was elected to Parliament in 1837. His controversial novel about the Chartist movement, Sybil, or The Two Nations, appeared in 1845. He went on to be British prime minister twice, in 1868 and from 1874

Why did Dickens write novels?

During Dickens' lifetime, reading was the most popular pastime at home, along with music-making, needlework, parlour games, such as Blindman's Bluff, and cards. This was an age before radio, film, and television. When Oliver is rescued from the streets by Mr Brownlow, Mrs Bedwin soon teaches him to play cribbage (an old fashioned board game). When Oliver enters Mrs Brownlow's study he finds "a little back-room, quite full of books . . . where the people could be found to read such a great number of books as seemed to be written to make the world wiser."

The urge to read

"'We won't make an author of you,' Mr Brownlow tells Oliver jokingly, 'while there's an honest trade to be learnt . . .'" Respectable or not, authors were impacting on society, both rich and poor. Despite the lack of proper schooling, most families had at least one member who could read, and he or she would read in the evening by the light of a candle or oil lamp. Dickens knew *Oliver Twist* would be read aloud in many homes, some of which might have no books other than a family Bible. For poorer readers, buying novels in magazine instalments was cheaper and therefore popular.

Oliver Twist was a huge commercial success. Drawings by Cruikshank featured on the front of this ten-part edition, and among the scenes shown is the death of Sikes (bottom right).

The painting *Dickens' Dream* by R W Buss (1804–1875) shows the writer surrounded by the characters Dickens' vivid imagination created. These fictional people became almost as real to him as his family and friends.

CENTURY OF NOVELISTS

Without other distractions, such as TV, computers and the Internet, people in Europe and the United States had time to read long novels. Many great novelists were writing in the 1800s. These included Scott, Austen, the Brontës, Thackeray, Trollope, George Eliot, and Hardy (Britain); Balzac, Hugo, and Flaubert (France); Cooper, Hawthorne, and Melville (US); and Dostoyevsky and Tolstoy (Russia).

Magazines gave readers news, opinions, facts, cartoons, and murder stories as well as serials. Leading artists such as George Cruikshank did the drawings for serials, and pictures put up in shop windows helped sell magazines. Dickens' serials were all-new stories, not reprints of old ones, so when reading *Oliver Twist*, people never knew what was coming next. Dickens began this new serial in *Bentley's Miscellany* magazine in February 1837, while still working on *The Pickwick Papers*.

George Cruikshank (1792-1878)

*George Cruikshank was the leading **satirical** artist of his day. Between 1837 and 1843, he did 126 illustrations for Bentley's Miscellany, including the pictures for Oliver Twist. Writer and artists worked closely. Dickens would send a section of text to Cruikshank or to the Pickwick artist, Hablot K Browne, who returned a drawing next day. Dickens would suggest small changes, and sometimes hurry to the artist's house to explain*

Rich and poor

In Britain, in 1820, 30 per cent of the population lived in towns and cities. By 1900, the figure had risen to around 80 per cent. In other countries, the US for example, more people lived in the country: in 1820 only seven per cent of Americans were city-dwellers, rising to 50 per cent by 1900. The rapid growth of Britain's towns, and the flow of country people to cities looking for work, led to severe overcrowding, poor **sanitation**, crime, and disease. For the poor, the choice was between filthy **slums** and the parish workhouse.

This illustration from *The Pictorial Times* of 29 August 1846 shows "A Poor Law Divorce". In the workhouse, married couples were forced to live apart.

Escaping the workhouse

In the 1830s, one in ten people in Britain were so poor they needed help. "We looked out for fresh bones . . . and then we used to be like . . . dogs over them", commented a hungry workhouse inmate at Andover, Hampshire, England. Under the new Poor Law of 1834, poor people could no longer turn to a local official for food and a few pennies.

TOWN AND COUNTRY

In Chapter Eight, Oliver sets out to walk to London, after seeing a milestone reading: 70 miles to London. "He had often heard the old men in the workhouse say that no lad of spirit need want in London; and that there were ways of living in that vast city which those that had been bred in country parts had no idea of." Oliver, still innocent, has no idea of what awaits him.

WHY CHANGE THE POOR LAW?

Under the new Poor Law system in England, the sick, the old, and the jobless were forced to live in workhouses where they were fed in return for work. The Poor Law Amendment Act of 1834 appointed three commissioners to supervise the new system. The intention was to save money and improve the system, but also to make workhouses so awful that people who were fit and well enough to work would stay out of them.

Instead, they were forced to work and live in a workhouse run by managers who rarely knew or cared for their charges. To escape the workhouses, tens of thousands of men and women drifted into begging, casual work, or crime in the fast-growing cities.

Charity or government welfare?

In Dickens' later story, *A Christmas Carol*, the **miser** Scrooge has a simple answer to the problem presented when "thousands are in want of common necessities". Refusing to give money to the poor, Scrooge retorts: "Are there no prisons, are there no workhouses?"

Giving to the poor through charity had been inadequate to meet the needs of so many. The 1834 Poor Law Act and its workhouses were a sign of change – the government started to take responsibility for welfare. But no government yet saw the need to spend taxpayers' money on the poor.

In the workhouse, many people lived only just above starvation level. In *Oliver Twist*, Dickens says that the workhouse managers "established the rule that all poor people should have the alternative . . . of being starved by a gradual process in the house [the workhouse], or by a quick one out of it." The old system did not work, and the new one was not much better.

The Flower Seller by Hilt (1862) shows two ladies leaving home to find a boy selling flowers in the street. Many poor youngsters earned a few pennies as street traders or beggars, hoping for charity from those more "fortunate".

21

Women in Dickens' world

In Dickens' time, few upper- or middle-class women had jobs, though working-class women worked hard on farms, in factories, and as servants. Most Victorian men thought a woman's place was at home, raising children. Pregnancy brought health dangers and many women died in childbirth (as does Oliver's mother). Women could not vote, and in reformer John Stuart Mill's phrase were "classed with children and lunatics [mentally ill people] as incapable of taking care of themselves".

GETTING AN EDUCATION

Although the 1842 Mines Act banned girls and boys younger than ten from working in Britain's coal mines, many girls still went to work rather than to school. Poorer girls might learn to read and write at a dame school, run by a childminder. Richer girls had lessons at home. A few girls were sent away to school. In the 1820s and 1830s, the three Brontë sisters, Charlotte, Emily, and Anne went to a boarding school in Yorkshire. All three became famous writers.

The care-worn expression of this mother shows how hard life could be for many Victorian women, exhausted by work and child rearing.

Married life

Dickens first fell in love in the late 1820s, but his feelings for Maria Beadnell were not returned. He married Catherine Hogarth in 1836. Catherine's sister Mary moved in with the newlyweds, and Mary's death in 1837 greatly affected Dickens. From 1842, the Dickens household included Catherine's other sister, Georgina. In 1858, Charles and Catherine separated, and, though less scandalous than divorce, marriage break-up was still relatively unusual. The previous year, Dickens had fallen in love with a young actress named Ellen Ternan, with whom he had a relationship until his death.

This drawing makes fun of women who wore the bell-shaped crinoline dresses of the time. The dress was worn over a cage-frame, here being blown up with bellows as maids struggle to get their mistress dressed.

Nancy and street-women

Women play key roles in *Oliver Twist*. Nancy is a prostitute, used by Fagin and Sikes to control and recruit boy thieves. Dickens was concerned for the well-being of prostitutes and helped set up Urania Cottage, a London refuge for women prostitutes who wanted to leave the streets. Despite her rough treatment by men, Nancy still has enough human feeling to care for Oliver and to help him escape a life of crime. She has the courage to stand up to Sikes knowing that it is dangerous. Her murder is so violent that even the thieves are shocked by it.

Nancy is an outsider, and Oliver's mother, too, was an outcast in the eyes of society because she had an **illegitimate** child. She dies soon after giving birth, and the nurse at her deathbed (who is drunk – nurses were commonly regarded as drunks in Dickens' day) mumbles about her own "thirteen children . . . and all on'em dead except two and them in the workus with me . . ." Older women in Dickens' books can be kindly motherly types, like Mrs Bedwin, but also **degraded**, like the nurse, or hard-hearted, like the Widow Corney (who bullies Mr Bumble) and Mrs Sowerberry (who feeds Oliver the dog's dinner).

PREGNANCY AND PAIN

Being born "illegitimate" (to an unmarried mother) was a social disaster in Victorian times, but common. Birth control was ineffective, and sexual knowledge often scanty. Unmarried girls who became pregnant often abandoned their babies. Many married women had numerous pregnancies, and painful births. Anaesthetics were pioneered in the 1840s – Queen Victoria was given painkillers at the births of the last two of her nine children.

A London School Board inspector and a police constable hunt out boys living rough, in order to get them into school. This picture appeared in the *Illustrated London News* in 1871.

Children in the city

When the Artful Dodger meets Oliver outside London, he says, in his strong London accent, "I've got to be in London tonight; and I know a 'spectable old genelman as lives there, wot'll give you lodgings for nothink". Oliver is happy to go with this new friend, and the Dodger heads straight for Saffron Hill – a district known to many readers of the time as having street thieves and **pickpockets**.

Children on the streets

Dickens was horrified by the number of street-children he saw in London. From 1821 to 1851, London's population doubled and there was not enough housing. People were flooding into the city, and many children were sleeping rough. Some were orphans or runaways. Others had been thrown out by their parents or employers, or had fled from workhouses. In the 1850s, around 30,000 children were living on London's streets. To buy bread, they sold matches, firewood, buttons, or bootlaces, cleaned shoes, ran errands, and swept away the dung dropped by the city's thousands of horses. Street-children were easy prey for criminals.

Dr Barnardo (1845-1905)

*Thomas Barnardo arrived in London from Ireland in 1866. He had planned to be a Christian **missionary** in China, but instead went to preach in the slum districts of the capital city. There he saw children sleeping in hay carts, in lofts, and in doorways. Determined to help them, in 1870 he set up a home to care for street-boys, and the organization he founded still works to help young people today.*

Dickens the reformer

To help slum children, Dickens demanded **reform**, and he found Angela Burdett-Coutts a useful friend. At the age of 23, she had become the richest woman in England, after her step-grandmother left her a vast fortune. Dickens encouraged her to fund schools for poor children, and refuges for London prostitutes. She also backed the London Society for the Prevention of Cruelty to Children. She and Dickens supported the Ragged School Union, a charity providing schools for "ragged" slum children. Robert Raikes, in the late 1700s, and John Pounds, in the 1820s, had pioneered ragged schools for the poor in Britain.

FACTS ABOUT FOOD

In the workhouse Oliver gets "three meals of thin gruel a day with an onion twice a week and half a roll on Sundays". This was deliberate exaggeration by Dickens. The official dietary, or food-allowance, approved by the Poor Law Commissioners in 1836, was bread, gruel, potatoes, a little meat, a little cheese, and one pudding a week on Fridays. Children over nine were fed the same as adult women, and children under nine were fed "at discretion", which often meant as little as possible.

Angela Burdett-Coutts (1814–1906) was a close friend of Charles Dickens who used her wealth to fund schools, homes for the poor, and for famine relief, especially in Ireland. She helped found the National Society for the Prevention of Cruelty to Children. It later became Britain's main child protection organization.

Going to school

Dickens' own schooling was interrupted by his parents' money problems. The 1834 Poor Law required local officials to see that poor children were taught to read and write, but few poor children in Britain got much education until after 1870. Schools charged fees. There were some well-run schools, but also many dreadful ones, which inspired Dickens to invent "Dotheboys Hall". In this school, which Dickens wrote about in his third novel *Nicholas Nickleby*, children were starved and abused, and taught practically nothing.

OFF TO SEA OR UP A CHIMNEY

The workhouse managers consider "shipping off Oliver Twist in some small trading vessel bound to a good unhealthy port . . . the probability being that the skipper would flog him to death, in a playful mood . . . " Workhouse children could be sent anywhere; to sea, or to climb chimneys for a chimney sweep. Oliver is spared such a fate by being "sold" for £5 to work for Mr Sowerberry the undertaker.

An innocent abroad

Mrs Sowerberry, wife of the undertaker in *Oliver Twist*, says she sees "no saving in parish children . . . for they always cost more to keep than they're worth". The young street thieves that Oliver later meets are uneducated, but experienced. They live by their wits, hoping to escape prison. Also, being "transported" (shipped to Australia, as there was no room in prisons) was a fairly typical punishment, even for minor crimes.

George Cruikshank drew this picture of a ragged school in Smithfield, London, around 1830. Several classes are being taught in the same room.

The RAGGED SCHOOL.
In West Street (late Chick Lane) Smithfield

Britain's private schools taught the sons of the gentry. Thomas Hughes' bestseller *Tom Brown's Schooldays* (1857), was about a boy at Rugby School. This illustration shows the hero Tom singing a country song to the applause of his school friends.

Schools for all

Readers of *Oliver Twist* were shocked to learn that many children lived like outlaws, with no schooling. There was a clear need for education reform, and not just in Britain. Massachusetts set up the first US state board of education in 1837, and Dickens wrote that Britain had much to learn from Massachusetts. Compulsory school attendance began with new state laws in the United States after 1850. In Britain, the Education Act of 1870 provided schools for five to eleven-year-olds at a small charge, but free state elementary education for all did not come until 1891.

Oliver Twist ends with Oliver starting lessons with a private tutor, like many better-off boys. It turns out that, despite being an orphan, Oliver comes from a better-off background. He also discovers that he will inherit money. Money, for Dickens, makes all the difference.

EVIDENCE FROM THE STREETS

In 1850, a boy named George Ruby, who worked as a London crossing sweeper, sweeping away the horse-dung and rubbish from the street, appeared in court as a witness. The judge asked him: "Can you read?"
"No"
"Do you know what God is?"
"No"
"What do you know?"
"I knows how to sweep the crossings."

Fagin in the condemned cell, where Oliver sees him "rocking himself from side to side, with a countenance more like that of a snared beast than the face of a man". In the book, Fagin does not escape punishment, but he does in the stage and film musical *Oliver!*

Anti-Semitism

After *Oliver Twist* was published, Dickens received some criticism from people who felt that in making one of the villains a Jewish person he was being **anti-Semitic**, a term used to describe prejudice directed against Jewish people. To describe Fagin as a "very old shrivelled Jew" sounds anti-Semitic to a modern reader. Dickens was writing in an age with different ideas about religious or racial discrimination. He explained later that he used the term "Jew" to describe a people, not a faith-group. In Victorian times, most Jewish people in Europe and the United States felt like outsiders in a mainly Christian society. At the time Dickens wrote *Oliver Twist*, the press often blamed Jewish moneylenders and criminal "masterminds" for London's crime.

DICKENS AND MRS DAVIS

In 1860, Dickens sold his house to a Jewish couple, Mr and Mrs Davis. They became friendly, and when Mrs Davis complained about the character of Fagin in a letter to the Jewish Chronicle newspaper, the author defended himself by saying that "it unfortunately was true of the time to which the story refers that that class of criminals almost invariably was a Jew". Dickens later wrote to her: "There is nothing but good will left between me and a people for whom I have a real regard and to whom I would not wilfully have given an offence or done an injustice".

PERSECUTION

*Jewish people in Europe had been **oppressed** for hundreds of years. In 1290, all Jews were expelled from England, but by the 1800s there were again small Jewish communities, mostly in cities. They played little part in public life, owing to restrictive laws, but were respected for their family values, business skills, hard work, and religious customs. But elsewhere in Europe, in Russia and Poland for instance, Jews were **persecuted**, and many left Europe as **migrants** to the United States.*

Fagin and Shylock

Fagin has not profited by crime. He lives in a slum, even though his house is full of stolen trinkets and silk handkerchiefs. He is "villainous looking", but Oliver sees him as a "merry old gentleman". He guards his stolen treasures in a hidden box, and is angry when Oliver sees him looking at his "pretty things". He tells Oliver that although people think he is a miser, the jewels are all he has to live on in his old age.

The most famous Jewish character in English literature before Fagin was Shylock in Shakespeare's play *The Merchant of Venice*, the merchant character who demands his "pound of flesh" (not letting someone off paying, even if it causes them pain). Shakespeare makes the audience feel sympathy for Shylock, and Dickens also shows a warmer side to Fagin's nature. He is the nearest thing the boy-thieves have to a father, and at the end of the story Oliver prays that Fagin be forgiven for his crimes.

Prisoners in the City Prison, Holloway, London, in 1862.
They are picking oakum (a plant fibre used to seal the planking of wooden ships), a common prison task. On the right is the **treadmill**, on which prisoners were made to walk for hours as punishment.

Dickens and his city

London, the city that so fascinated him, was Dickens' home for many years. In 1837, he had set up home at 48 Doughty Street, in Mecklenburgh Square, moving to a larger rented house at 1 Devonshire Terrace, his home until 1851. He also owned Tavistock House in Tavistock Square, London, and a country house, Gad's Hill Place, in his favourite county of Kent, southeast of London.

London's streets were full of horses and horse-drawn carts. Rich people had private carriages, but most people walked to work, and walked between villages (now city suburbs) to visit relatives and friends. Dickens walked for miles, usually alone and often at night. As he walked, he was tracing the footsteps of earlier writers such as Daniel Defoe and Henry Fielding who had had written about London's vibrant street life, and its lawless backstreets.

DISEASE AND DEATH

*Thousands of Londoners had died during the **cholera** outbreak of 1832, and there were to be four other outbreaks of this killer disease in Dickens' lifetime. Better public health and sanitation eventually reduced its threat. Many other diseases claimed lives, too. The average age of death in London was only 27 years old. Almost half the funerals in London in 1839 were of children under ten.*

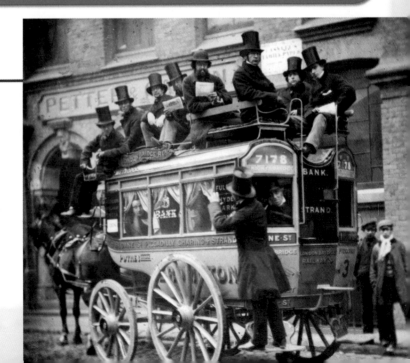

This photograph from about 1865 shows Londoners in "stovepipe" hats on a horse-drawn bus. Passengers inside had a little more comfort than those braving the weather on the open-top seats.

A map of Dickens' London. Dickens walked many miles through its main streets, squares and back alleys, gathering material for his novels and observing the city's mix of people.

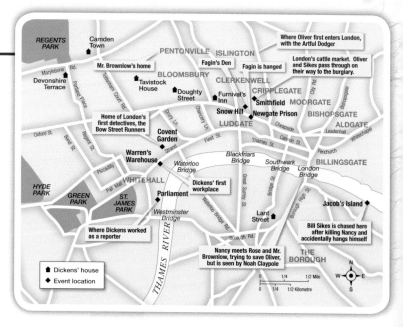

A map of Dickens' London showing:

- REGENTS PARK
- Camden Town
- Where Oliver first enters London, with the Artful Dodger
- PENTONVILLE
- ISLINGTON
- Mr. Brownlow's home
- Fagin's Den
- Fagin is hanged
- London's cattle market. Oliver and Sikes pass through on their way to the burglary.
- Marylebone Rd.
- Devonshire Terrace
- BLOOMSBURY
- CLERKENWELL
- Portland Place
- Tottenham Court Rd.
- Tavistock House
- Doughty Street
- Furnival's Inn
- CRIPPLEGATE
- MOORGATE
- City Rd.
- Bishopsgate
- Oxford St.
- Bond St.
- Regent St.
- Home of London's first detectives, the Bow Street Runners
- Drury Lane
- Chancery Lane
- Snow Hill
- Smithfield
- Newgate Prison
- BISHOPSGATE
- LUDGATE
- Cheapside
- Leadenhall
- ALDGATE
- Whitechapel
- Covent Garden
- Strand
- Fleet St.
- Thames St.
- Gracechurch St.
- Fenchurch St.
- Warren's Warehouse
- Blackfriars Bridge
- Southwark Bridge
- London Bridge
- BILLINGSGATE
- Piccadilly
- Waterloo Bridge
- Great Surrey St.
- Bridge St.
- HYDE PARK
- GREEN PARK
- ST. JAMES PARK
- WHITEHALL
- Pall Mall
- Dickens' first workplace
- Parliament
- Westminster Bridge
- Waterloo Bridge Rd.
- Borough High St.
- Jacob's Island
- Lant Street
- Bill Sikes is chased here after killing Nancy and accidentally hangs himself
- Where Dickens worked as a reporter
- THAMES RIVER
- Borough Rd.
- THE BOROUGH
- Nancy meets Rose and Mr. Brownlow, trying to save Oliver, but is seen by Noah Claypole
- ■ Dickens' house
- ◆ Event location
- 0   1/4   1/2 Mile
- 0   1/4   1/2 Kilometre

Backstreet life

It was unwise for respectable citizens to enter certain districts of London, unless armed or with a companion. One of the worst "crime-dens" was Saffron Hill, where it was said all the pocket-handkerchiefs stolen by all the pickpockets in the city fluttered from windows. There were many public houses, or taverns, where crooks like Bill Sikes could be found "skulking uneasily through the dirtiest paths of life . . ." as Dickens put it in his preface to *Oliver Twist*. Neglected children were easily tempted into crime by girls like Nancy, hanging around pubs such as "The Three Cripples".

Child criminals

In this darker London, children learned to pick pockets. Oliver enters this world when, guided by the Artful Dodger, he climbs the "dark and broken stairs" to Fagin's den, where "the walls and ceiling were perfectly black with age and dirt". Yet even here there is a little cosiness too: sausages frying in a pan on the fire, bread and butter, and a group of boys smoking clay pipes and "drinking spirits with the air of middle-aged men". Crime supports this underground community. Drying by the fire are "a great number of silk handkerchiefs", stolen by the boys, and ready to be sold.

This is how Dickens describes the Saffron Hill district (near Camden Town), as Oliver follows the Artful Dodger towards his first meeting with Fagin:

Covered ways and yards, which here and there diverged from the main streets, disclosed little knots of houses, where drunken men and women were positively wallowing in filth . . .

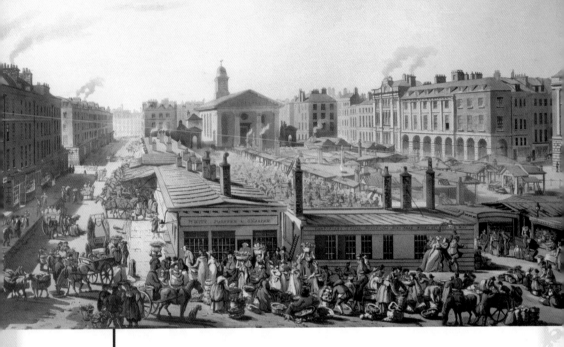

Covent Garden Market, *Bird's Eye View*, Ackerman (1811).
London's main vegetable market was in Covent Garden until it
was moved to a new site in 1974.

JUSTIFYING HIS WORK

Dickens knew that Oliver Twist might upset some readers, because "some of the characters in these pages are chosen from the most criminal and degraded of London's population". He explained his motives in his Preface, or introduction, to the book. He said he had often read about "amiable" thieves, but never encountered "the miserable reality". Showing the criminal underworld realistically would "be to attempt something which was needed and which would be a service to society".

Observing the underworld

As a reporter, and on his walks through the city, Dickens observed the life of the streets: the drunks, the ragged children sleeping in corners, the prostitutes, the street sellers, musicians, and entertainers. "A dirtier or more wretched place he had never seen . . . There were a good many small shops, but the only stock in trade [things shops sold] appeared to be heaps of children . . . crawling in and out of the doors, or screaming from the inside." This is how Oliver Twist first sees the murky backstreets of London, after meeting the Artful Dodger.

London was the government and commercial centre of Britain's Empire. In the 1830s, its new railways were still only in the planning stage, sailing ships still berthed in the docks, and districts still had trades dating from the Middle Ages. The Haymarket, for example, still drew in farmers in hay wagons, and Covent Garden (originally a monks' garden) was the city's main fruit and vegetable market.

Jacob's Island

After sunset, gaslights glimmered in the smarter squares, but many streets were unlit apart from a flickering oil lantern. It seemed darkest beside the River Thames, foul smelling because of the sewage and waste tipped into it every day.

Ships packed the docks downstream of London Bridge, and there was a constant flow of shipping along the waterway, as busy as the narrow streets of the city. Bill Sikes, on the run after the murder of Nancy, flees to Jacob's Island, in Southwark, a district of houses built on mud, surrounded by water and reached by wooden bridges.

Dickens called it "the filthiest, the strangest, the most extraordinary of the many localities that are hidden in London".

London's underworld was revealed to a wider public through books such as *Oliver Twist*, and also by the reporting of journalist Henry Mayhew, who told street-people's stories in their own words in his articles and books.

Henry Mayhew (1812–1887)

Henry Mayhew was the founder of the humorous magazine Punch. *His extra work as a campaigning journalist showed the serious side of his nature, as a social reformer. He wrote a series of "snapshots" in words, interviewing Londoners, roaming the streets to talk to them, and writing down their own accounts of how they lived. Among the people he met were street-boys, bird-sellers, road-sweepers, conjurers, actors, rat-catchers, beggars, and a Moroccan street-trader.*

Crime and punishment

The criminals in the London underworld led by Fagin are very different from the innocent Oliver. On his first morning with them, after a breakfast of coffee, hot rolls, and ham, Oliver begins his "education" in crime. He is so innocent that the other boys laugh at him, but laughter dies when Fagin asks whether there was "much of a crowd at the execution that morning". Public hangings were still seen as entertainment.

Learning to steal handkerchiefs from pockets becomes a game, with Fagin the teacher, Oliver the pupil, and the other boys the skilful experts. Fagin compliments Oliver: "if you go on in this way, you'll be the greatest man of the time." What Oliver does not know is that Fagin is part of a plot to turn him from innocence to crime.

The burglary at Chertsey, from Chapter 22 of *Oliver Twist*. During the break-in, Oliver is shot by "two terrified, half-dressed men". Watching from the scullery window, Bill Sikes is about to haul the boy out by his collar and escape into the night.

SENSATION OR INFORMATION?

*Dickens said he wrote Oliver Twist to show the truth about crime in London. He knew he risked upsetting readers, calling the book a "hazardous experiment". Some critics might object to the **sensational** treatment of crime and murder, and complain the book was unfit to be read by respectable people. But Dickens felt that by writing about "low life", he could spark new discussion about social reform, and about crime and punishment.*

Harsh punishments

Until 1808, a pickpocket like the Dodger would have been hanged. The law was harsh, and over 200 crimes carried the death penalty at that time. Though the British Prisons Act of 1835 set up a new system of inspecting prisons, most jails were old, overcrowded, and foul. Many prisoners were kept chained or made to turn a treadmill. Many prisons did not reform. A pickpocket, aged fifteen, told Henry Mayhew (see page 33): "I have been in prison thirteen times in all. Every time I came out harder than I went in. I've had four floggings [beatings], but when I got out I soon forgot it."

When Oliver is arrested, the magistrate Mr Fang seems like a bully and a fool, ready to punish the innocent as well as the guilty. Fang was based on a real magistrate, Mr Laing, whom Dickens had seen in court. Laing was eventually dismissed from his job.

LONDON'S FIRST POLICE FORCE

When the British politician Sir Robert Peel proposed a city police force for London, opponents of the idea argued that such a force would damage "that perfect freedom of action and exemption from interference which are the greatest privileges and blessings of society in this country..." Nevertheless, the new Metropolitan Police force was set up in 1829. Other countries set up police forces, too. New York City had one by 1845.

Cops and robbers

Bill Sikes, the burglar, has little to fear from police, and is ready to attack, beat, and murder for just a few pennies or a silver watch. Until 1829, law enforcement in London was carried out by local constables and by the **Bow Street Runners**. Most citizens locked their doors at night and many kept a gun to defend their property. Oliver is shot during a break-in planned by Sikes.

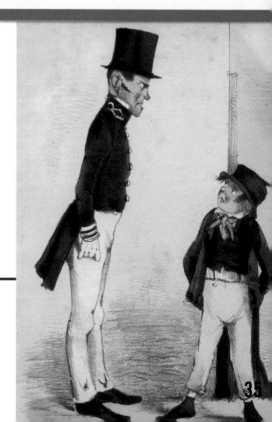

London's new police were not very popular. In this 1830 cartoon, a loitering youth is asked "what are you up to?" He retorts that he is "waiting for the young gal wot I pays my attention to".

Changing times

The London that Dickens described in *Oliver Twist* was disappearing even as he wrote. Brick buildings and railways were replacing old wooden houses and cobbled streets. The stagecoaches and cosy inns of Mr Pickwick's adventures were already old-fashioned. The slums of London lasted longer. Many were not cleared until after Dickens was dead, and some remained into the 1900s.

Arguments rage

This age of change sparked fierce arguments about what kind of society was emerging. Dickens was in favour of change if it made life better for the weak and underprivileged. Yet he was also conservative: he wished to keep some things unchanged. He believed in the old ideals of self-help, of hard work, discipline, and making your own way. But he was also in favour of new government ideas to improve public health, housing, and education.

DIFFERENT FUTURES

*Dickens thought people could change. Noah Claypole, the bully from the undertaker's shop, does not – he ends up as an **informer** and **conman**. One of Fagin's boys, Charley Bates, does change. He gives up crime and, after much hardship and struggle, becomes "the merriest young grazier [a farmer who raises and fattens cattle] in all Northamptonshire".*

Britain was the first country to experience the full blast of the Industrial Revolution. This is the northern steel-making city of Sheffield in Yorkshire, in 1884. Smoking chimneys and glowing furnaces symbolized the new age.

Backing the weak

Because Dickens cared about the weak and oppressed, he approved of the campaign, led by William Wilberforce in Britain, to end the slave trade. Slavery was an issue of dangerous controversy in the United States, where **abolitionists** clashed with slave-owners. This clash would erupt into the **Civil War** of 1861–1865. Dickens disliked the ideas of economists such as Thomas Malthus who believed people must "sink or swim" without government help. Dickens feared this meant the strong would grow stronger at the expense of the weak.

TRAVELLING AT SPEED

As a young reporter, Dickens travelled in a horse-drawn carriage, "writing on the palm of my hand, by the light of a dark lantern . . . at the surprising rate of fifteen miles an hour." In 1830 the world's first steam railway, between Liverpool and Manchester, brought travel at twice that speed. Some doctors feared the human body would collapse under the strain! But the steam railroads were a huge success.

The modern world

Dickens lived to see railways bring cheap travel to all. He used the train to commute between Folkestone, in Kent, and London, and was involved in a rail crash at Staplehurst in 1865. In his lifetime, too, the electric telegraph brought rapid message sending between Europe and the United States. Society changed more slowly; women did not win the right to vote until the 1900s in Britain and the United States. But women did gain new rights in property ownership and marriage, and began moving into professions, such as medicine.

The rail crash at Staplehurst in Kent in June 1865. The crash had a deep effect on Dickens, and he was never quite the same again.

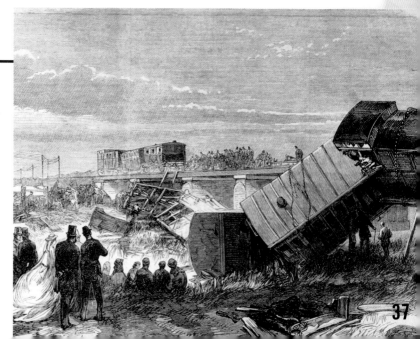

Books make celebrities

Dickens made news with his books, and also through lecture tours and readings, and trips to Europe and the United States. He was a literary celebrity, and very soon there were others. For example, Mark Twain, the American writer, became wealthy and famous enough to set up his own publishing firm in the 1880s.

Publishers and copyright

Before the 1800s, publishing and bookselling had been the same trade, but in Dickens' lifetime publishing books became separate from selling them. Publishers competed to find new authors. After 1710 in Britain, an author's work was protected by **copyright** laws; a book was the property of the author or the publisher, and could not be copied by anyone else. Although the United States had had a copyright law since 1790, US publishers for some time sold illegal copies of books by British authors, which meant the authors received no money. This obviously annoyed authors such as Dickens. The United States gave no copyright protection to foreign authors until 1891, after Dickens had died.

CHILDREN'S BOOKS

Dickens always wrote with children in mind, knowing his books would often be read aloud in the family. Yet when he was a boy, children's literature was made up mostly of alphabet books, ABCs for reading, and stories with a simple moral. There were very few picture books. This changed in the later 1800s, when popular writers for children included Louisa M Alcott (Little Women), Anna Sewell (Black Beauty), Robert Louis Stevenson (Treasure Island), and Lewis Carroll (Alice's Adventures in Wonderland).

Dickens enjoyed relaxing in the country near Rochester, Kent. In 1856 he bought Gad's Hill Place, and it was in this house that he died in 1870.

A *Family Gathering*,
a typical Victorian domestic
painting, by Joseph Clark.
A father reads to the family
beside the fire.

A tide of words

In Europe and the United States, printing presses churned out a growing number of books, newspapers, journals, and magazines. Fiction, such as novels, made up only a small part of this output. Most of the books were non-fiction and included books about science, religion, geography, and history. Of 45,000 books published in Britain between 1816 and 1851, only 3,500 were fiction titles.

Books were sold from street stalls as well as by bookshops. People also borrowed books from libraries, paying a small fee every time, but so great was the demand for books that free public libraries soon opened. One of the first free public libraries, paid for by taxes, was started in Peterborough, New Hampshire in the United States in 1833. The first public libraries in Britain opened after 1850.

Dickens the journalist

As well as briefly being a newspaper editor (of the *Daily News* in 1846), Dickens edited two successful weekly journals: *Household Words* (from 1850) and its successor, *All the Year Round*. As well as serializing his later novels, he also wrote many shorter stories and essays, and encouraged other writers, such as Mrs Elizabeth Gaskell. His journals became famous for their Christmas editions, selling over 300,000 copies each.

MASS LITERACY

Only the better-off, like Mr Brownlow, could afford a private library at home, but British reading surveys in the 1840s revealed that even in northern coal-mining villages most people could read and write at least a little. Only one person in five could neither read nor write.

Other writers of the time

Dickens grew up at a time when the **Romantic Movement** inspired many writers and artists. By the mid 1800s, two opposing views were often clear in writing, and in art. Some artists looked back wistfully to the past. Some painters, for example, drew on the Middle Ages for inspiration. Others looked forward, with optimism, using scientific discoveries as the basis for thrilling adventures, such as French writer Jules Verne in his fantasy novel *From the Earth to the Moon*.

First among equals

Dickens' extraordinary imagination, and hard work, lifted him above his fellow writers. Before Dickens, the most popular novelist was Sir Walter Scott, author of historical adventure stories such as *Ivanhoe*. Also popular were the US authors James Fenimore Cooper (*Last of the Mohicans*) and Washington Irving (*Rip Van Winkle*). Jane Austen, author of *Pride and Prejudice*, is now ranked with Dickens, but he never thought much of her writing style.

William Makepeace Thackeray (1811–1863)

William Makepeace Thackeray was almost as popular as Dickens. He was the author of Vanity Fair, *which was published in 1847. Thackeray was a brilliantly witty critic of society. Unlike Dickens, he had a university background. He was easy-going and his friends said he was easier to get along with than Dickens.*

UNCLE TOM'S CABIN

A book that had a great impact on society in the 1800s was Uncle Tom's Cabin. Written by Harriet Beecher Stowe it was published 1851–1852, and also turned into a play. It was a story of African-American slaves in the United States that helped mobilize opinion against slavery – so much so that Mrs Stowe was hated in the southern slave-owning states. She was congratulated by abolitionists, and received a warm welcome when she visited Britain.

135,000 SETS, 270,000 VOLUMES SOLD.

UNCLE TOM'S CABIN

FOR SALE HERE.

AN EDITION FOR THE MILLION, COMPLETE IN 1 Vol, PRICE 37 1-2 CENTS.
"   "   IN GERMAN, IN 1 Vol, PRICE 50 CENTS.
"   "   IN 2 Vols, CLOTH, 6 PLATES, PRICE $1.50.
SUPERB ILLUSTRATED EDITION, IN 1 Vol, WITH 153 ENGRAVINGS,
PRICES FROM $2.50 TO $5.00.

The Greatest Book of the Age.

Dickens' success helped other writers, as it created a demand for novels. Many were three-volume love stories that were very long, and often lacking inspiration. But there were new trends, including science fiction, the horror stories of Edgar Allan Poe, and detective stories. Dickens was a friend of Wilkie Collins, author of some of the first detective novels in English literature (*The Moonstone*, *The Woman in White*). Collins worked on Dickens' journal *Household Words* and the two writers travelled around Europe together. Collins, unlike Dickens, was untidy and lazy, but nevertheless Dickens and he got on well.

Dickens' circle

Other writer friends of Dickens included the US poet Henry Wadsworth Longfellow (who wrote "The Song of Hiawatha"), William Harrison Ainsworth (author of *Rookwood,* a story about the English highwayman Dick Turpin), and Elizabeth Gaskell, whose novels include *North and South*. While he encouraged Mrs Gaskell, Dickens was rude about another British woman writer, George Eliot. He called her and her partner George Henry Lewes "the ugliest couple in London". Dickens read novels by Charlotte and Emily Brontë (*Jane Eyre* and *Wuthering Heights*). Unlike Dickens, the Brontë sisters stayed out of the limelight. Their books were first published in 1847, using male pen-names because it was thought "unladylike" for respectable women to write novels.

After *Oliver Twist*

Like other authors of the day, Dickens ended *Oliver Twist* with a farewell to his characters: "I would fain linger yet with a few of those among whom I have so long moved . . ." The success of *Oliver Twist* gave Dickens confidence to tackle other themes. While the public continued to demand "novels of the lowest character" (about crime and murder) as one 1830s commentator remarked, Dickens could choose his own subjects for future books.

Dickens and the United States

On his visits the United States, Dickens was impressed by a fresh attitude to problems: "the state is a parent to its people", he wrote. Americans, he thought, believed in progress, and especially in education, and he liked the way rich Americans gave money to fund schools and libraries. He made a particular friend in Cornelius Felton, professor of Greek at Harvard University, and the son of poor parents who had done well through hard work.

THE ST. GEORGE'S SOCIETY'S DINNER AT DELMONICO'S, ON 23D APRIL, 1857.

Dickens received a warm welcome on his return to America in 1868. He toured the major cities and attended banquets such as this one at "Delmonico's" in New York City.

Fame brought its own pressures. In the United States, in 1842, Dickens complained of all the attention:

If I turn into the street, I am followed by a multitude. If I stay at home, the house becomes, with callers, like a fair . . .

THE AUTHOR AS STAR

After Oliver Twist, Dickens was a star. He was rather vain, combing his hair often and fussing about his clothes. He liked rooms with mirrors to reflect not only the candlelight, but also him. He enjoyed fame and was proud of his membership of the exclusive Garrick Club in London, which is still a favourite club with actors.

Dickens also enjoyed visiting Italy and Switzerland. On one such trip, he began *Dombey and Son* – the first of the series of great novels that established his reputation: *David Copperfield*, *Bleak House*, *Little Dorrit*, *A Tale of Two Cities*, and *Great Expectations*.

Dickens the showman

Even though Dickens was popular, his books still sold far fewer copies than the hundreds of thrillers featuring highwaymen, cowboys, pirates, runaway lovers, scandals, and exotic travels that were published every year. Dickens the showman responded to this sensation-seeking public with dramatic readings. A favourite performance was the murder of Nancy from *Oliver Twist*, which became a highlight of his exhausting reading tours. Audiences fell silent at the closing words as Sikes, having beaten Nancy to her knees, cuts short her final prayer for mercy: "The murderer staggering backward to the wall, and shutting out the sight with his hand, seized a heavy club and struck her down."

Dickens worked so hard, and made so many tours to give public readings from his books that his health suffered. By 1870 he looked like an old man, though he was only in his late fifties. While working on *The Mystery of Edwin Drood* at his home on 9 June 1870, he collapsed and died of a stroke.

This 1861 photograph of Dickens shows him about to give one of his famous public readings, book and baton in hand.

A caricature (exaggerated drawing) by André Gill (1868) shows Dickens crossing the ocean, as an international star.

Dickens' reputation

By Dickens' death in 1870, *Oliver Twist* had become a classic. Though few critics called it Dickens' best book, most people knew the outline of the story. But by the start of the 1900s, Dickens' reputation had begun to sink. Although his books were still popular, critics found them out of touch with modern life. Times change, and so do reading tastes. Dickens is now, once again, admired for his achievements, for his range of characters and language, and his social concerns.

Dickens on stage

There were stage versions of *Oliver Twist* almost as soon as the last instalment had appeared, early in 1839. Dickens gave different voices, gestures, and facial expressions to every character. He developed this technique by acting out passages on his own. Not all the Victorian stage versions of *Oliver Twist* were successes, however – one closed in under a week. Theatre producers cut the social criticism and simply told the story with as much drama as possible.

REFORMERS AND CAMPAIGNERS

Books such as Oliver Twist helped to inspire campaigners including:
- *Jane Addams (1860–1935) who founded Hull House in Chicago for poor **tenement** dwellers*
- *Josephine Butler (1828–1906) who cared for prostitutes in Britain*
- *Octavia Hill (1838–1912) a campaigner for better housing*
- *William and Catherine Booth, who founded the Salvation Army in 1865 to "sweep the gutters and seek the lowest".*

LIE-DOWN PROTEST

During one stage performance of Oliver Twist, Dickens lay down on the floor of his theatre box, refusing to watch! He wanted to put on his own version, starring leading actor William Charles Macready, but Macready said no. After this, Dickens decided to stick to novels.

Dickens on the screen

Films of Dickens' stories have usually made a lot of the social comment, which interests modern audiences. The film of *Oliver Twist* made by David Lean in 1948 was shot in black and white, to highlight the shades between good and evil. It starred Alec Guinness as a crafty Fagin. In 2005, Roman Polanski filmed the story, with Ben Kingsley as Fagin.

Lionel Bart's musical show *Oliver!*, which was first staged in the 1960s, and then filmed, added colour and light – and cut several leading characters. In the musical, Fagin emerges as a witty rascal rather than a wicked criminal (he escapes at the end), and even the backstreets and taverns glow with life and fun.

This shot from David Lean's 1948 film of *Oliver Twist* shows the workhouse children lining up for gruel.

Opening doors for other writers

Dickens' success made it easier for later writers about "real life" to succeed. Among them were US writers Stephen Crane, Theodore Dreiser, Frank Norris, and James T. Farrell. Many authors who write about city life may owe part of their success to Dickens. Three examples are:

- Damon Runyon – his New York street-stories inspired the musical *Guys and Dolls*
- Kristin Hunter – her 1960s story *The Soul Brothers and Sister Lou*, was about life in an inner-city ghetto
- Michelle Magorian – her novel *Goodnight Mr Tom* tells of an abused boy from the city who finds a friend during World War II.

A "Penny Black" stamp. All British postage stamps since this first issue have showed the head of the reigning monarch (king or queen). When the penny post was introduced in 1840, Victoria had been queen for just three years.

Did *Oliver Twist* change history?

Oliver Twist got more people talking about Britain's poverty and crime problems. Dickens opened the public's eyes to the misery of London's slums, and the way children in particular were affected by poverty and crime. From 1840 campaigners in Britain could use the new **penny post** to pressure the government and inform the public. The government was pressed into making reforms.

The poor are always with us

Despite the positive response to his book, the abuses that Dickens had revealed did not go away. There were still poor people, slums, and crime. Fear of the workhouse encouraged workers to form "friendly societies", associations into which each person paid a little every week, as a form of insurance against unemployment or sickness. Anyone who lost his job or who fell ill could ask the society for help, and stay out of the workhouse.

In Britain, old-age **pensions** paid for from taxes started in 1908. In 1911, a system of national health insurance was begun, to give sick pay to any worker too ill to work. The workhouse slipped from the pages of history, even though the British government was still making changes to the Poor Law in 1930, and the law itself was not finally abolished until 1948.

The welfare debate

In the United States, the welfare system, which had at first been very like the system in Britain, developed as a mix of state and federal government aid. During the **Great Depression** of the 1930s, so many people were jobless and homeless that a new Social Security Act was passed in 1935. The new law gave the government more responsibility to help children, disabled people, the elderly, and the unemployed.

The United States has never gone as far as Britain, or some other European countries, in having a tax-funded welfare state in which the government takes responsibility for relieving poverty and providing health care. In the United States, as in most countries, the question of how poverty, social deprivation, and crime are best tackled is still a subject of debate, among politicians and the public.

BETTER OR WORSE?

*Dickens' friend, Thomas Carlyle, was a **pessimist**. He felt that the world was getting worse. But another great novelist of the era, Anthony Trollope, felt things were getting better. In 1883, Trollope said he was pleased to see "how comfort has been increased, how health has been improved, and education extended".*

Queen Victoria (1819–1901). Victoria became Britain's queen in 1837, a month after her eighteenth birthday. The young queen had read *Oliver Twist*, which she found "too interesting". Here she is shown reading in later life.

What is the message of *Oliver Twist?*

Oliver Twist survives because he is innocent. He asks for more, and eventually gets it. Many experts would have predicted that, given his upbringing and experiences among the criminals, Oliver should have "turned bad". But he does not. He remains good despite what happens to him.

BORN TO A LIFE OF CRIME

Dickens suggests that chance decides whether people sink into crime, or live lawfully. Nancy tells Rose: "Thank heaven that you had friends to care for and keep you in your childhood . . ." But when Rose begs her to seek a new life, Nancy replies that she cannot leave Bill. "I am drawn back to him" she says, "through every suffering and ill usage."

Villains

Dickens writes with sympathy about some of his villains, especially Nancy, Fagin, and the Artful Dodger. He tries to show how they think, and what motivates them. Monks, by contrast, is more like a "stage-baddie" who is there to advance the plot. In jail, Fagin gets a prayer of forgiveness from Oliver, but there is no compassion for Sikes – even the murderer's dog turns against him at the end.

Dickens wrote of *Oliver Twist* that, however shocking his book was, it was the truth, showing "the best and worst shades of our nature". The new Poor Law had aroused "a great deal of indignation", and as for the new workhouses, "it may be rather faintly hoped that *Oliver Twist* had some effect in improving them." Dickens was not too hopeful, however.

By the end of the 19th century, every child was receiving a basic education. This photo (about 1900) shows girls studying plants at a London school. The reform movement had triumphed, though there was still much to be done.

FAREWELL TO FAGIN

In the death cell, Fagin tells Oliver where to find the papers about his birth and legacy "in a canvas bag, in a hole a little way up the chimney". Then Oliver leaves the condemned man, passing through the crowd gathered outside the prison to watch the hanging. "Everything told of life and animation [activity], but one dark cluster of objects in the centre of all – the black stage, the cross-beam, the rope, and all the hideous apparatus of death." Public executions in Britain ended in 1868; the death penalty was abolished in the UK in 1969.

Changes

In 1851, W. M. Thomas wrote in Dickens' journal *Household Words* that "old haunts of dirt and misery" were being replaced by "new slums". Much of the city Dickens knew was destroyed by bombs during World War II (1939–1945) or redeveloped afterwards. Though workhouses have been replaced by modern welfare payments, social problems, such as child abuse, street crime, prostitution, and violence, remain. Rather unfairly perhaps, the term "Dickensian" is sometimes used to mean "old-fashioned", and not always in a complimentary way.

Judgement

The message of *Oliver Twist* is that the individual matters. *Oliver Twist* ends happily for Oliver, but shadows loom from the gallows hanging over Fagin. The novel ends in a church, in which a memorial tablet bearing the name "Agnes" has been placed for Oliver's dead mother. Dickens writes that surely her spirit will revisit that "solemn nook", and find forgiveness (in Heaven) "because she was weak and erring". It was the reassuring ending most readers expected.

Oliver, now a young gentleman, and Rose Maylie contemplate the memorial to his mother. The final paragraph gave his book the sentimental and religious ending Dickens felt most readers wanted.

TIMELINE

1812	Charles Dickens born on 7 February.
1812	Britain and United States at war in the War of 1812.
1821	Boston opens the first US public high school.
1822	The Dickens family move to London.
1827	Dickens leaves Wellington House Academy in London, and starts work as a clerk in a lawyers' office.
1829	Foundation of London's police force.
1830	Liverpool and Manchester Railway opens in Britain. It is the first steam-hauled passenger railroad.
1830	Dickens starts work as a Parliamentary reporter.
1832	The Great Reform Bill, to give the vote to more people (but not all) is passed in Britain.
1833	Dickens publishes his first story, anonymously.
1833	Factory Act in Britain bans children under nine from working in textile factories.
1834	Dickens starts using the pen-name "Boz".
1834	The Poor Law Amendment Act in Britain changes the rules for workhouse admission and treatment.
1836	Dickens and Catherine Hogarth marry, 2 April.
1836-1839	*Oliver Twist* is published as a magazine serial.
1837	Victoria becomes queen of Britain.
1837	Mary Hogarth dies suddenly.
1837	US state of Massachusetts sets up a state board of education for public schools.
1842	Mines Act in Britain stops girls, and boys under ten, from working underground in coal mines.
1842	Dickens visits the United States for the first time.
1844	Factory Act limits children under thirteen to working 6½ hours a day.
1847	Ten-Hour Act in Britain reduces working day for women and children under eighteen to no more than 58 hours a week.
1847	Michigan is first US state to abolish the death penalty.
1850	US population tops 23 million. 15 per cent live in cities.
1850	Dickens begins editing his weekly magazine-journal, *Household Words*.

KEY	World history
	Local/national history (United Kingdom)
	Author's life
	Oliver Twist

1851	Dickens buys Tavistock House in London, and fits out one room as a private theatre.
1852	First compulsory schooling legislation in the United States, in state of Massachusetts.
1856	First US kindergarten, a private nursery school started in Watertown, Wisconsin.
1857	Dickens falls in love with Ellen Ternan, whom he has met while acting in a play written by his friend Wilkie Collins.
1858	Charles and Catherine Dickens separate.
1859	Dickens starts a new magazine-journal, *All The Year Round*.
1861	Start of Civil War in the United States.
1865	Dickens and Ellen Ternan escape death in a railway accident in Kent.
1865	London's new sewerage scheme is finished. Octavia Hill sets up a housing scheme for the poor in London.
1865	Freedom of all slaves in the United States.
1868	New laws allow local councils in Britain to demolish unsanitary homes (slums).
1868	Dickens visits the United States for the second time.
1869	US population now almost 39 million, with 25 per cent living in cities.
1870	British Education Act sets up school boards to provide schools for five- to eleven-year-olds, for a small charge.
1870	First home for homeless London boys opened by Thomas Barnardo.
1870	Death of Charles Dickens.
1875	Public Health Act in Britain sets new minimum standards for clean homes, especially ventilation and drains.
1884	The British National Society for the Prevention of Cruelty to Children is founded. Britain's first law to prevent cruelty to children is passed by Parliament.
1891	New law in Britain makes free primary schooling for all children compulsory.
1935	Social Security Act in the United States to ease Depression poverty.
1948	Poor Law is abolished following the foundation of 'welfare state" in Britain, with no-charge-for-use medical and education services.
1969	Death penalty abolished in Britain.

FURTHER INFORMATION

The edition used in the writing of this book is *Oliver Twist*, Heron Books, with introduction from Oxford Illustrated Dickens, Oxford University Press.

Other works by Charles Dickens

The Pickwick Papers (1836-1837)
Oliver Twist (1837-1839)
Nicholas Nickleby (1838-1839)
The Old Curiosity Shop (1840-1841)
Barnaby Rudge (1841)
Martin Chuzzlewit (1843-1844)
A Christmas Carol (1843)
Dombey and Son (1846-1848)
David Copperfield (1849-1850)
Bleak House (1852-1853)
Hard Times (1854)
Little Dorrit (1855-1857)
A Tale of Two Cities (1859)
Great Expectations (1860-1861)
Our Mutual Friend (1864-1865)
The Mystery of Edwin Drood (unfinished)

Books about Dickens, the Victorians, and *Oliver Twist*

Blincoe, Robert, *The Real Oliver Twist* (Icon Books Ltd, 2005)
Dickens, Charles Jnr, *Dickens's Dictionary of London 1888: An Unconventional Handbook* (Old House Books, 1995)
May, Trevor, *The Victorian Workhouse* (Shire Publications Ltd, 1997)
Ross, Stewart, *Dickens and the Victorians* (Hodder Wayland, 1986)
Williams, Brenda, *Victorian Children* (Heinemann Library, 2003)
Williams, Brenda, *Victorian Homes* (Heinemann Library, 2003)
Williams, Brenda, *Victorian Jobs* (Heinemann Library, 2003)
Williams, Brenda, *Victorian Women* (Heinemann Library, 2003)

Useful websites

www.heinemannexplore.co.uk
For information on the Victorians
www.dickensmuseum.com
Website of Dickens House Museum in London
www.victorianlondon.org
Background on the city Dickens knew
www.victorianweb.org/history
Timeline of British law-making on social issues
www.online-literature.com/dickens/olivertwist
Background on the writer and his book

Places to visit

Dickens House Museum, 48 Doughty Street, London
Dickens Birthplace Museum, 393 Old Commercial Road, Portsmouth
London Museum, London

Films

Oliver Twist (2005)
Directed by Roman Polanski and starring Barney Clark and Ben Kingsley, this version of the film has been highly praised.
Oliver Twist (1985)
Musical adaptation by Lionel Bart, directed by Gareth Davies and starring Ben Rodska and Eric Porter.
Oliver! (1968)
This musical version, directed by Carol Reed, stars Ron Moody and Mark Lester.
Oliver Twist (1948)
The black and white classic, directed by David Lean, stars Robert Newton and Alec Guinness.

GLOSSARY

abolitionists people who were against slavery and wanted it stopped

anti-Semitic prejudiced against Jewish people

apprentice young person who is taught a trade by an experienced craftsman or "master"

beadle parish officer, in Dickens' time, who was responsible for welfare

biographer author who writes the life story of another person

Bow Street Runners organization of detectives and thief-catchers in London from the 18th century until 1829, operating from Bow Street magistrates' court

Chartist supporter of voting reform in Britain in the 1830s and 1840s. The Chartists, mostly working men, drew up a list or Charter with their demands.

cholera dangerous infectious disease carried by bacteria in polluted water

Civil War war between the Northern and Southern states of the United States, 1861-65

conman dishonest person who sets out to cheat or trick others out of money

copyright legal protection of a person's work or idea from being copied by someone else

degraded brought down, debased and disgraced, made to seem worthless and lowered in dignity by living in a morally or physically unpleasant way

frowzy untidy and dirty

Great Depression economic downturn after the financial crisis that hit America in 1929. It affected world trade and led to mass unemployment in the 1930s.

idealize imagine something is ideal

illegitimate describes someone born "out of wedlock" – to an unmarried mother

Industrial Revolution changes in manufacturing beginning in the 1700s with new machines for spinning and weaving, and the first steam-driven machines

informer person who gives information, usually about criminals to the police

legacy money or property left to someone by a person who has died, under the terms of a will

migrant person who moves from one country to another in search of work or to settle

miser a person who hates to spend money

missionary person who preaches and teaches his or her religious beliefs to others

motives aims and ideals that drive a person to carry out a project or to behave in a certain way

oppressed treated cruelly or unfairly by others, or by a government

parish workhouse hostel for poor, homeless people, paid for by the local parish – a small church and local government district

pen-name name used by a writer to disguise his or her real identity

penny post first national system for sending mail using pre-paid stick-on postage stamps, begun in Britain in 1840 – the first stamps cost one penny

persecute pick on someone or some group deliberately, to expose them to mean, cruel or vicious treatment or even to kill them

pensions money paid to old and retired people

pessimist someone who believes that things get worse, not better. (The opposite of an optimist.)

pickpocket thief who steals from people in the street – taking things from their pockets or bags

pioneer person who is among the first to do something

poor law British system from the 16th-20th century for providing poor people with work and shelter

privies old-fashioned non-flushing toilets – usually a hole in the ground

prostitute someone performing sexual acts for money

reform to make better, or to turn someone from bad habits

reformer person who tries to change the law to improve things

revolution overthrow of a government or great change in how things are done

Romantic Movement intellectual and artistic movement of 1700s to 1800s that looked for inspiration in nature and human imagination

sanitation clean and safe disposal of toilet waste

satirical something that makes fun with a serious intent to point out evil, wrongdoing or foolishness; a satirical book or picture is funny but has a point

sensational arousing strong emotions or sensations, causing a stir amongst the public

serial story that appears in episodes or instalments, like a TV "soap"

slums areas of bad housing, lacking proper sanitation or clean water

smallpox disease that is no longer a threat, but was a killer before the mid 1900s

social conscience caring about the rights and responsibilities of people, and about the humane and fair government of society

squalid dirty, wretched and miserable

stagecoach enclosed carriage pulled by horses

tenement a city building made up of rooms to rent

treadmill hollow wheel inside which a prisoner was forced to walk, so turning it, as a punishment

vice sin or immoral behaviour

workhouse local institution in the 19th century for the poor, homeless and jobless, providing food and a bed in return for work

INDEX

Ainsworth 41
anti-Semitism 13, 17, 28-29
Arnold, Dr Thomas 14
Austen, Jane 40

Barnado, Dr Thomas 24
Brontë sisters 22, 41
Burdett-Coutts, Angela 25

Carlyle, Thomas 10, 47
Chartists 16, 17
child labour 9, 11, 16, 26
childbirth 22, 23
children's literature 38
Christmas Carol, A 21
city-dwellers 20
Collins, Wilkie 41
copyright laws 38
Covent Garden Market 32, 33
crime 10, 12, 21, 26, 28,
    31, 32, 34-35, 48
Cruikshank, George 13, 18,
    9, 26

David Copperfield 9
death penalty 34, 35, 49
Dickens, Charles
    celebrity status 6, 38,
        42, 43
    early life 8-9
    marriage and children 6,
        7, 9, 22
    public readings 6, 43
    theatrical talents 4, 6, 44
    writing career 6, 9, 39,
        42, 43
disease 20, 30
Disraeli, Benjamin 16, 17
Doré, Gustave 5

Eliot, George 41
emigration 17, 29

factory work 16
family values 15
friendly societies 46

Gad's Hill Place 6, 30, 38
Gaskell, Elizabeth 39, 41

Hogarth, Mary 15, 22
housing 5, 36, 44, 49
Hughes, Thomas 27

illegitimate children 23
Industrial Revolution 5, 36

Jacob's Island 33
journalism 9, 39

literacy 39
Little Dorrit 8
London 5, 11, 24, 30-33,
    36, 49

Maclise, Daniel 15
magazines 4, 9, 18-19
Malthus, Thomas 37
Mayhew, Henry 33, 35
Mill, John Stuart 22

National Society for the
Prevention of Cruelty to
    Children 25
Nicholas Nickleby 26
novelists 19, 38, 40-41, 45

Oliver Twist 4, 5, 6, 7,
    10-35, 42, 43
    adaptations 44, 45
    storyline 12-13
    style and themes 5, 10-35,
    46, 48, 49

pensions 46, 55
The Pickwick Papers 9, 19
Poe, Edgar Allen 41
police 35
Poor Law 7, 10, 14, 20, 21,
    25, 26, 46, 48, 50
Pounds, John 25
poverty 7, 10, 11, 20, 46, 47
prisons 8, 29, 35
prostitution 5, 23, 25, 44,
    55
public libraries 39, 42
publishing business 38-39

ragged schools 25, 26

Raikes, Robert 25
railways 17, 37
reading habits 18, 19, 39
River Thames 14, 33
Romantic Movement 40, 55

Saffron Hill 31
Salvation Army 44
schools 25, 26-27, 48
Scott, Sir Walter 40
serial publication 4, 9, 15,
    18, 19
Shakespeare, William 29
slave trade 37, 41
social reform 7, 16, 25, 33,
    36, 44, 46
steam power 17, 37
Stowe, Harriet Beecher 41
street-children 24, 26

Ternan, Ellen 22
Thackeray, William
Makepeace 6, 40
transportation 26
Twain, Mark 38

underworld 5, 10, 31, 32,
    33, 34
United States 5, 7, 8, 11,
    16, 17, 20, 27, 29, 35,
    37, 38, 39, 42, 44, 47

Verne, Jules 40
Victoria, Queen 4, 16, 23,
    38, 47
voting rights 16, 22, 37

welfare system 46, 47
Wilberforce, William 37
women 22-23, 37, 41
workhouses 7, 12, 20, 21,
    25, 26, 46, 48